NEVER ALONE
POETRY MEETS FAITH.

- ERNST LOUIS -

Book Design and Book Cover Design by Ernst Louis.
Book Cover Illustration by Mannayah Louis
Illustration photos are from pixabay.com
and from Ernst Louis.

Publisher: RelaSonship LLC
Dacula, GA 30019
Number of pages: 177
Made in the USA
12-9-2020

DEDICATION:

"But to all who did receive Him,
to those who believed in His name,
He gave the right to become
children of God."

John 1:12 BSB

*M*ost joyfully, gratefully, and humbly I dedicate
this book to God, my Heavenly Father, the Author
and faithful Sustainer of my soul and my family.

SPECIAL HONOR:

"Jesus said unto her,

'"I am the resurrection, and the life:

he that believeth in Me,

though he were dead,

yet shall he live.'"

John 11:25 KJV

It is with humility and deep gratitude that I honor the memory of my father, Hebert Louis, and my mother, Loriette Beaussicot. I am profoundly grateful for their selfless love and sacrifice. May they rest in God's love and peace; and may their reward be great.

SPECIAL THANKS:

Special thanks to you, dear reader, for reading my work. It is my
sincere hope that you will be inspired, refreshed, and encouraged.
May you always taste and see the Lord's goodness.

FOREWORD:

I enjoy poetry that strengthens my faith and makes me feel secure and never alone. It can mean many things to many people. Poems can be the lighting of a candle in times of darkness. They can express inspirations in nature; flowers, trees, animals, clouds, rainbows, lakes, rivers, streams, mountains, valleys, rain, snow, a cool summer breeze, the sun, the moon and many other beautiful God breathe things.

The poems in this book exemplify God's gifts to mankind. As the words of these poems dance across your mind, I hope they will be inspiring to you.

Eardine Reeves Lee
Author of "A Teacher's Story"
CEO of Banbury & Nickleby's
www.banburyandnicklebys.com

CONTENTS:

Foreword vi

Never Alone 1

Your Love 3

I Am Only Clay 5

It's Wonderful 7

I Choose You 9

Thank You Abba 11

No Better Lover 13

Retrospect 15

In You Jesus 17

Heavenly Father 19

Folly 21

Conversation From the Pit 23

Still I Smile 25

Smile Anyway 27

It's Going to be Okay 29

Awake in the Dream of Life 31

I Think You Think 33

No One Would Know 35

We Are Not Going Anywhere 37

He Died and Rose 39

The Baptizer 41

The Lord's Train 43

Blessed Are Those.. 45

Children of the Journey... 47

Watchers of the Night.. 49

Behold Eden.. 51

My Ardent Plea.. 53

Souls Passing Through.. 55

The Big Picture.. 57

Jesus and Spring.. 59

Freedom.. 61

I Am Zacchaeus 63

The Truth.. 65

Tell Me The Truth.. 67

Lies.. 69

Transparency.. 71

Exposed.. 73

Divine Remedy.. 75

The Best Gift.. 77

My Place in the Son.. 79

Faith Renewal... 81

Never Mind.. 83

Homage to God's Lamb... 85

Rock N Roll 87

God is in Control 89

Remember Lot's Wife... 91

Letting Go.. 93

Feelings & Faith... 95

Never Too Far............. 97

God Our Pillow.. 99

To His Will I Bow.. 101

Did God Have His Way?....................................... 103

Clock Wise... 105

It's Time... 107

Spare Me.. 109

Let Money Be... 111

The Only Pure Source.. 113

True Words to Live By.. 115

Let Love... 117

Love.. 119

The Fruit of the Spirit.. 121

The Bell of Love Rings.. 123

Love Moved Out... 125

A Little Pondering.. 127

Delightful Morning.. 129

Look and Listen.. 131

Consider the Sparrow... 133

Summer... 135

Where Wild Flowers Grow................................... 137

Rest... 139

What About Us?... 141

Haiku Inspector... 143

Relaxation... 145

Elevate... 147

Evolving Evil.. 149

My Child... 151

You Matter... 153

I Will Make it Through.. 155

Your Attention Please... 157

Atlanta... 159

Be Ready to Fly... 161

To Be in God's Presence... 163

About the Author.. 165

Blessing... 166

"Let all that you do be done in love."

1 Corinthians 16:14 ESV

NEVER ALONE.

Led by Your Spirit,
in a world of hate,
but I don't fear it,
though I feel its weight.

I am not alone,
Your strength is with me;
although I bemoan,
all the pain I see.

Help me shine your light,
show the lost Your way,
so wrongs be made right,
this I humbly pray.

Let ev'ry heart know,
Your presence is near;
make this world below,
a place without fear.

Dearest God of love,
may all taste and see,
Your grace from above,
and a new world be.

"Do not fear, for I am with you; do not be afraid, for I am
Your God. I will strengthen you; I will surely help you;
I will uphold you with My right hand of righteousness."

Isaiah 41:10 BSB

YOUR LOVE.

Nothing I've seen before,
deep as the ocean floor,
is Your love. Your love.

High above all the earth,
none can measure the worth,
of Your love. Your love.

Forever pure and true,
faithful through and through,
is Your love. Your love.

Displayed for all to see,
upon a tree for me,
was Your love. Your love.

So much stronger than death,
supplying ev'ry breath,
is Your love. Your love.

Giving me faith and hope,
to stand trials and cope,
is Your love. Your love.

Holding me through the night,
oh Bright and Morning Light,
is Your love. Your love.

"Behold what manner of love the Father has given to us,
that we should be called children of God.
And that is what we are!"

1 John 3:1a BSB

I AM ONLY CLAY.

I am only clay,
empty, dry, and poor;
looking for life's way,
I knock on Your door.

I am only clay,
needy, marred and weak,
asking You each day,
in my life to speak.

I am only clay,
to You I must come;
fashion me I pray,
I yearn to become.

I am only clay,
make me as You will;
help me not to sway;
cause me to be still.

I am only clay,

sitting at Your feet;

I am here to stay,

oh, You are so sweet.

I am only clay,

in the Potter's hand;

to me come what may,

I will firmly stand.

I am only clay,

made whole by Your word;

and now this I say,

I'm glad You're my Lord.

〜〜

"O house of Israel, cannot I do with you

as this potter?" saith the LORD.

"Behold, as the clay is in the potter's hand,

so are ye in mine hand, O house of Israel."

Jeremiah 18:6 KJV

IT'S WONDERFUL.

It's wonderful to know You are there,
when on Your name I call.
It's wonderful to know You care,
about all my troubles, great or small.

When haunted by the ghosts of the past,
when overwhelmed with my needs,
on You I then my cares cast;
for Your faithfulness always succeeds.

It's wonderful to know You understand,
when no one else does,
and that You and I, hand in hand,
will conquer all my foes.

It's wonderful to know You know,
the end from the beginning.
Your favor You will surely show,
to all who serve You as King.

It's wonderful and delightful,
Your kindness, love and grace.
You are wonderful, and I am thankful,
that one day I will see Your face.

"God is our refuge and strength,
a very present help in trouble."

Psalm 46:1 KJV

I CHOOSE YOU.

From the proud You hide Your face,
but to the meek You show Your grace.
I would be a hopeless fool to choose pride,
and forfeit Your sweet presence by my side.

When life's a blur and answers hard to find,
who am I to lean on my own limited mind?
The heart is inclined to evil and full of lies;
hence I dare not in my own eyes be wise.

Light of the world, illuminate my path,
guide and keep me from the day of wrath.
Jesus my Lord and Great High Priest,
help me to stand and resist the evil beast.

The world tells me to always follow my heart;
this road leads far from You right from the start.
I refuse to lose my soul for passing pleasures,
giving You up and all Your eternal treasures.

～～

"Trust in the LORD with all your heart,
and do not lean on your own understanding.
In all your ways acknowledge Him,
and He will make straight your paths.
Be not wise in your own eyes;
fear the LORD, and turn away from evil."

Proverbs 3:5-7 ESV

THANK YOU
ABBA.

Thank you Abba for always being there for me.
Through my confusion, tears and restlessness,
through my doubts and fears, still my eyes see
and my mouth tastes Your glorious goodness.

Father, never once have you forsaken my soul;
time and time again Your love comes through.
When life gets tough and the trials take a toll,
You calm my heart, reminding me to trust You.

Your love remains, in spite of all my wrongs;
I am perplexed, humbled, and in absolute awe.
Words are not enough, even in all the tongues,
to articulate Your gracious love without a flaw.

So when the storms come upon my life's boat,
and the waves rush over to sweep me away,
I will rest in my Father's love to stay afloat,
and sing to You delightfully without delay.

"For I know the thoughts that I think toward you,
saith the LORD, thoughts of peace,
and not of evil, to give you an expected end."

Jeremiah 29:11 KJV

NO BETTER LOVER.

There is no better lover than You Lord;
there is nothing truer than Your word.
When my heart grows hard and cold,
I run to Your love that is purer than gold.

Lately the trials have greatly intensified;
cynicism, selfishness, strife, sadly glorified.
Long ago, of all these things You did foretell;
lawlessness increasing, this surely rings a bell.

Lord, let not my heart partake of this toxicity;
please keep it pure and ever near Your proximity.
Fill me with Your Spirit, Your very own essence,
so I can truly reflect Your wonderful presence.

Strengthen my frail faith and cause it to endure;
loving Anchor of my soul, in You I am secure.
Wash and purify my heart from sin's soil,
and help me not become the devil's spoil.

Beloved Lord, I know that You will soon return;
to be with You is what my heart does yearn.
Come quickly Lord to bring the joy of salvation,
to a dying humanity, Your dearly loved creation.

"Be strong, and let your heart take courage,
all you who wait for the LORD!"

Psalm 31:24 ESV

RETROSPECT.

I remember it so well,
the place, the despair and hell;
the agony, the sorrow, the brokenness,
the pain, the tears, and tenderness;
the day when unto You I cried,
longing for my soul to be satisfied.
As a child cries when in pain or in need,
I cried unto God, my soul to feed.
Somehow I knew to call You Father;
although You are my God and Maker.
You heard me from Your holy place,
and upon me bestowed Your grace.
You have saved me from my despair;
Your love to me has been so fair.
You picked me up when I did fall,
You are my God, my friend, my all.
Oh, how can I ever forget,
the day when my need was met?
Yes, I remember it so well,
the day You rang my heart's bell.

"In my distress I called upon the LORD,
and cried unto my God:
He heard my voice out of His temple,
and my cry came before Him, even into His ears."

Psalm 18:6 KJV

IN YOU
JESUS.

In You I have a new and divine nature,
by Your Spirit I am made a new creature.
In You I have a promising and eternal future;
for You indeed are my green pasture.
In You I find joy and pleasure,
life and peace without measure.
When all around me seems obscure,
You are the Light that makes me secure.
May my soul grow strong and mature,
as my spirit feeds on your Holy Scripture,
and when I am in doubt and unsure,
may I remember that Your love is pure.

"His divine power has given us everything we need
for life and godliness through the knowledge of Him
who called us by His own glory and excellence.
Through these He has given us His precious
and magnificent promises, so that through them
you may become partakers of the divine nature,
now that you have escaped the corruption
in the world caused by evil desires."

2 Peter 1:3-4 BSB

HEAVENLY FATHER.

As I watch the prophecies unfold,
as lawlessness grows manifold,
just as Your Son foretold,
in days of old;
as I journey through this world so cold,
Your lovely face may I behold,
my right hand I pray You hold,
and make me strong and bold;
my whole being I pray You mold,
so to this world my soul never be sold,
and may I seek You more than the purest gold.

"Do not love the world or anything in the world.

If anyone loves the world,

the love of the Father is not in him."

1 John 2:15 BSB

FOLLY.

Folly, I despise you, but truth be told,
you are enticing and lovely to behold.
You were Adam and Eve's big mistake;
of your poisoned delight I won't partake.

Folly, you are the eternal forbidden fruit,
enchanting like the sound of the flute,
but you are to my soul the kiss of death,
you, the skillful robber of man's breath.

Folly, getting rid of you is proving to be hard;
don't you know from my life you are barred?
I know how this ends, I won't take the chance;
no, you may not, and will not have this dance.

Folly, you keep ringing my heart's door bell,
because you know my Achilles' heel too well;
but I resist you, you evil child of Lucifer;
thus, to my Heavenly Father's wisdom I defer.

'The woman Folly is loud;

she is seductive and knows nothing.

She sits at the door of her house;

she takes a seat on the highest places of the town,

calling to those who pass by,

who are going straight on their way,

"'Whoever is simple, let him turn in here!'"

And to him who lacks sense she says,

"'Stolen water is sweet,

and bread eaten in secret is pleasant.'"

But he does not know that the dead are there,

that her guests are in the depths of Sheol.

Proverbs 9:13-18 ESV

CONVERSATION
FROM THE PIT.

You thought you were being pious and brave,

while foolishly digging up your own grave;

now you are restless in your miserable pit,

and so afraid you will never come out of it.

Mr. Devil, I presume you have not yet heard

His magnificently excellent and loving word;

He is with me even when I lay my bed in hell,

therefore I can say, with my soul it's all well.

Seeking His righteousness isn't foolish at all,
though one may stumble, though one may fall.
He didn't say there'd be no hurdles on the way,
I know He's with me, regardless what you say.

Very well then, but why serve such a master
who holds from you what I'd give much faster?
I require not at all any virtue, but only your soul;
take my hand and let me pull you from this hole.

It gains one naught to lose the core of his being;
but you are too proud to see what I am seeing.
You can't love a soul, for you know not its worth;
this joy belongs only to the Maker of the earth.

From His own essence He created humanity;
to which you've brought misery and insanity.
But soon He will return and you will be no more;
your work He will undo, His work He will restore.

"Submit yourselves therefore to God.
Resist the devil, and he will flee from you."

James 4:7 ESV

STILL I SMILE.

You may well smear my name,

in your quest to bring me shame;

but still I stand and still I smile,

in spite of all your schemes so vile.

You may work hard to see my fall,

but I'm held by God who's my all.

So, still I stand and still I smile,

in spite of you, you lying reptile.

You hunt me like your favorite prey,

but my God will have the final say.

So, still I stand and still I smile,

in spite of your snares and your guile.

You knocked me down so very hard;
though I'm broken, though I'm scarred,
yet still I stand and still I smile,
for God is with me in every trial.

You thought for sure it was the end of me,
but I have been rescued handsomely.
So, still I stand and still I smile;
Keep scratching your head, it'll be a while.

"Consider it pure joy, my brothers,
when you encounter trials of many kinds,
because you know that the testing
of your faith develops perseverance.
Allow perseverance to finish its work,
so that you may be mature and complete,
not lacking anything."

James 1:2-4 BSB

SMILE
ANYWAY.

I know that you are hurting;
I mean not to dismiss your pain,
but please allow me to say,
your smile is not necessarily fake,
just because you are suffering.

See your smile as a lovely emblem,
one of resilience and courage,
your badge of honor and strength,
a bold statement of your will,
one that says "I will survive,
and will rise from the pit of despair."

Your smile does not have to mean all is well,
when this could not be further from the truth.
Your smile is not there to fool you, or others;
it is your ray of hope that says to yourself,
your ray of hope that tells the world,
that life is a gift to appreciate, rain or shine.

"Rejoice in the Lord always.
I will say it again:
Rejoice!"

Philippians 4:4 BSB

IT'S GOING TO BE OKAY.

The sky was looking quite moody today;
as if it was sad and wanted to cry.
Expectedly it burst into a river of tears;
then suddenly the sun peeked through
the thick, dark blankets of clouds,
and a rainbow appeared with a smile
to remind me once more,
it's going to be okay.

"Though the fig tree should not blossom,
nor fruit be on the vines,
the produce of the olive fail
and the fields yield no food,
the flock be cut off from the fold
and there be no herd in the stalls,
yet I will rejoice in the LORD;
I will take joy in the God of my salvation."

Habakkuk 3:17-18 ESV

AWAKE
IN THE DREAM
OF LIFE.

I am not quite sure how I ended up here,

in this shallow and illusionary place,

permeated with confusion, compromise and fear;

where life moves so fast, that I cannot keep pace.

It moves faster here than the Autobahn in Germany.

Welcome to superficiality on the Broadway of Broadways;

where the sky is the limit and the choices are many,

but despised are those who truly love the Ancient of Days.

Here they say "deprive not your soul of any pleasure;
you owe it to yourself to do whatever makes you happy."
"There is no specific order and there is no measure,
release your fears and simply be all that you want to be."

Everything seems to shine like gold on the surface,
until you probe beneath and see the mold and decay.
The innocence of life has vanished without a trace,
as hypocrisy, greed and vanity prevail night and day.

I would walk a thousand miles for one genuine smile;
I would climb the tallest mountain to meet one true friend,
but I must be patient and love everyone, meanwhile,
as I await the Lord's return, as I await until the end.

"And because lawlessness will be increased,
the love of many will grow cold.
But the one who endures to the end will be saved."
Matthew 24:12-13 ESV

I THINK
YOU THINK.

I think you think that I bleed blue,
I think you think I'm not like you;
unknown to pain and sorrow,
without care about tomorrow.

I think you think that I'm on crack,
I think you think I'm out of whack;
you want to wipe that smile off my face,
cause I'm not from the human race.

I think you think I have no clue,
I think you think I don't know you;
we're not that different from each other,
you're my long distance sister or brother.

I think you think you know more than I do,
I think you think this must be true;
your views may well differ from mine,
I love and respect you, that's my bottom line.

"To start a quarrel is to release a flood;
so abandon the dispute before it breaks out."

Proverbs 17:14 BSB

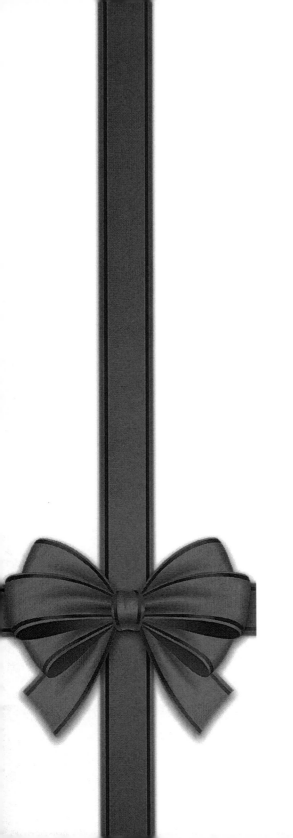

NO ONE WOULD KNOW.

No one would know,
wrapped up in a bow,
are morality trashers,
and proud God bashers.

No one would know,
wrapped up in a bow,
are covert hate dealers,
and false world healers.

No one would know,
wrapped up in a bow,
are manufacturers of lies,
parading in disguise.

No one would know,
wrapped up in a bow,
are children of confusion,
drowning in deep delusion.

No one would know,
wrapped up in a bow,
are despisers of light,
who are full of spite.

No one would know,
wrapped up in a bow,
are the know-it-alls,
authors of perilous falls.

No one would know,
wrapped up in a bow,
are innocence stealers,
and true hope killers.

No one would know,
wrapped up in a bow,
are lovers of vanity,
destroying humanity.

"Let the wicked forsake his way,
and the unrighteous man his thoughts;
let him return to the LORD,
that He may have compassion on him,
and to our God, for He will abundantly pardon."
Isaiah 55:7 ESV

WE ARE NOT GOING
ANYWHERE.

We are not going anywhere,
until the Lord returns for us.
We will meet Him in the air;
we will be with King Jesus.

Until then, we are here to stay;
for with our God we cannot lose.
Regardless what they do or say,
we will preach heaven's good news.

To the darkness, we daringly speak,

proclaiming Jesus as the Light.

We work hard to help the weak,

so they may stand up in God's might.

We go to remote places of the earth,

to reach out to the poor and rejected;

though they're deemed to have no worth,

yet upon them His face is reflected.

But we're called backwards and haters,

because we stand for Yahweh's ways.

We must not bow to these agitators,

who proudly flaunt their sins these days.

We've been despised through the ages;

we've been fed to lions and burnt alive.

They would have us gone from life's pages,

still we remain, we multiply, and thrive.

"And I tell you, you are Peter,

and on this rock I will build my church,

and the gates of hell shall not prevail against it."

Matthew 16:18 ESV

HE DIED AND ROSE.

For the blind and the lame,
He died.
For the sake of His name,
He died.
For the love of us all,
He died.
To lift up from the fall,
He died.
To conquer sin and death,
He died.
To give man endless breath,
He died.
To restore the Garden,
He rose.
To renew sweet Eden,
He rose.
To prepare the big feast,
He rose.
For the great and the least,
He rose.
To become her Husband,
He rose.
To love her without end,
He died and rose.

"And He began to teach them that the Son of Man must suffer many things and be rejected by the elders and the chief priests and the scribes and be killed, and after three days rise again."

Mark 8:31 ESV

THE
BAPTIZER.

I stand calling by the river,
like faithful John the Baptizer;
like thunder, or like whisper,
with a message to deliver.

From all your sinful ways–repent,
before your life is fully spent;
God's love for you will not relent,
until the firmament is rent.

Then closed will be the door;
mercy, alas–will be no more;
justice He surely won't ignore;
order He must and will restore.

Realize now you must decide,
to keep or let go of your pride;
yes you can run, but you can't hide,
from the One who for you died.

Upon us now is the end game,
no longer life will be the same;
It's time to trust and call His name,
and receive that for which He came.

I stand calling from the river,
with this message from life's Giver;
I stand ready in the water,
to bring you back to the Father.

"In those days John the Baptist came
preaching in the wilderness of Judea,
"'Repent, for the kingdom of heaven is at hand.'"

Matthew 3:1-2 ESV

THE LORD'S TRAIN.

Chugga chugga choo choo,
the love train is coming through.
Chugga chugga choo choo,
the Lord's train is here for you.

It's headed back to the garden of Eden,
where the tree of eternal life is hidden;
we will find no pain and sorrow there,
neither brokenness, violence, nor despair.

Come along, hurry, please don't be late.
Get on now, get on now, you mustn't wait.
Long ago your seat has been reserved;
for this trip your soul has been preserved.

Turning away this chance is a mistake;
understand your eternal destiny's at stake.
Be brave to leave your past behind you;
let it all go, your life will be made new.

"You don't know what I have done," you say;
that is true, still the Lord loves you anyway.
This train's been around crossing many waters,
bringing back home His sons and daughters.

Don't you worry one bit about the fare;
let go of your doubts, this you must dare.
Take no time to blink, no time to sneeze;
"stand clear of the closing doors please."

He brought you in, now look at you,
from every place, language and hue.
Welcome aboard mesdames and misters,
welcome indeed brothers and sisters.

Chugga chugga choo choo,
the love train did come for you.
Chugga chugga choo choo,
the Lord's train carried you through.

"But God proves His love for us in this:
While we were still sinners, Christ died for us."
Romans 5:8 BSB

BLESSED
ARE THOSE.

Blessed are those who for God's wisdom thirst.
Blessed are those who seek His kingdom first.
Blessed are those whose hope is in the Lord.
Blessed are those who cling to His faithful word.

Blessed are those who choose love over hate.
Blessed are those who choose the narrow gate.
Blessed are those who are now called the least.
Blessed are those who reject the mark of the beast.

Blessed are those who walk the narrow path.
Blessed are those who escape the coming wrath.
Blessed are those who look unto the risen Son.
Blessed are those who revere the Holy One.

Blessed are those who are meek and wise.
Blessed are those whom God does not despise.
Blessed are those who embrace His grace.
Blessed are those who will see His face.

"Enter through the narrow gate.
For wide is the gate and broad is the way
that leads to destruction,
and many enter through it.
But small is the gate and narrow the way
that leads to life, and only a few find it."

Matthew 7:13-14 BSB

CHILDREN OF THE JOURNEY.

Children of light,

children of might,

we are.

Children of the day,

children of the Way,

we are.

Children from above,

children born of Love,

we are.

Children from near and far,

children of the Saving Star,

we are.

Children of the Risen Son,

children of the Holy One,

we are.

Children of divinity,

children of infinity,

we are.

Children of destiny,

children of the journey,

we are.

"For you are all children of light,

children of the day.

We are not of the night or of the darkness."

1 Thessalonians 5:5 ESV

WATCHERS OF
THE NIGHT.

Watchers of the night,
keepers of the flame,
radiate His light;
and lift up His name.

Watchers of the night,
gaze upon the Son,
keep Him in your sight;
lest you come undone.

Watchers of the night,
singers of God's praise,
His children by right;
sing to Him always.

Watchers of the night,
keepers of the gate,
keep your fire bright,
for the hour's late.

Watchers of the night,
be strong and steady,
pray with all your might;
make His kingdom ready.

Watchers of the night,
ushers of the morning,
fight on the good fight;
soon you'll see your king.

"Watch and pray that you may not enter into temptation.
The spirit indeed is willing, but the flesh is weak."

Matthew 26:41 ESV

BEHOLD
EDEN.

Here comes the Son,
in all His might;
darkness be gone,
let there be light.

Honor His name;
let go of greed,
for pride and fame,
there is no need.

Evil must cease,
so must strife, too;
let there be peace,
for me and you.

Gone be the past,
goodbye sorrow;
freedom at last,
bright tomorrow.

Sweet as a dove,
our brand new start;
now there is love,
in every heart.

Behold Eden,
as it should be;
God's great garden,
eternally.

"He will wipe away every tear from
their eyes, and death shall be no more,
neither shall there be mourning,
nor crying, nor pain anymore,
for the former things have passed away."

Revelation 21:4 ESV

MY ARDENT
PLEA.

Lord, there is nothing good in me,

I am broken, needy and lowly,

yet, You think of me continually.

Lord, I know I am not worthy,

nor will I ever so be,

yet, You love me flawlessly.

Lord, Your love has set me free,

You have opened my eyes to see

that You are with me constantly.

Lord, in You I find my true identity;
be my vision, my dreams and destiny;
grant me to dwell with You eternally.

Lord, hear now my ardent plea,
more of Your pure essence in me;
for this I yearn more sincerely.

~

"For I know that nothing good
dwells in me, that is, in my flesh.
For I have the desire to do what is right,
but not the ability to carry it out."

Romans 7:18 ESV

SOULS
PASSING
THROUGH.

We are souls passing through.
We will all leave this world behind;
there is a better place for me and you,
where we will find perfect peace of mind.

It is called heaven, our eternal home.
In our Father's house there are many mansions;
Jesus Himself will all His children welcome,
to paradise, a place of numerous dimensions.

We are souls passing through.
Our hearts must cling to the everlasting!
Eternity awaits me and you;
forever we will reign with our King!

We are souls passing through.
We have tasted and seen that the Lord is good;
we must stay on the path that is true,
and despise wickedness, hatred, and falsehood.

We are souls passing through.
We must choose to love and turn from strife;
the will of our Father you and I must do;
Jesus is the Way, the Truth, and the Life.

"For we are strangers before you
and sojourners, as all our fathers were.
Our days on the earth are like a shadow,
and there is no abiding."

1 Chronicles 29:15 ESV

THE BIG PICTURE.

Come, come all of you who thirst,
and learn to seek God's virtues first.
Drink from His pure and holy fountain,
you'll gain strength to move any mountain.

Set not your heart on things below;
that which is true you must follow.
Why striving for what does not satisfy?
Why do you pursue that which is a lie?

"Vanity of vanities, all is vanity!"
All will pass away, that's the reality.
Take heed, lest that which you cherish,
become the cause for your soul to perish.

The grass is truly greener on the Lord's side;
He bids you to come and there abide.
He promised to make everything new;
fulfillment and lasting satisfaction await you.

Don't you know this system will soon cave in?
Why make "this way of life" your safe haven?
There's only one Way, one Life, Christ Jesus,
the Truth who was, is, and will be there for us.

"But whoever drinks of the water that
I will give him will never be thirsty again.
The water that I will give him will become in him
a spring of water welling up to eternal life."
John 4:14 BSB

JESUS
AND SPRING.

Jesus is like the season of spring;

new life and new beauty He'll bring—

to all stripped and lifeless trees,

by way of His warm and gentle breeze.

Splendidly the once dead becomes alive;

the barren and the broken now can thrive.

His sweet aroma fills the atmosphere;

Jesus, as spring is undoubtedly here!

Some find it very hard to believe

that the dead could again live;

some find it even foolish and odd,

but such is every great act of God.

Amazingly the old is now made new,
by God's promised and sent Heavenly Dew.
As the spring, Jesus is so lovely and fair,
to Him I'd dare no one compare.

He is present in summer, winter, fall;
He's always there when on His name I call.
He truly is my spring and my everything;
He is my beautiful song to forever sing.

⌣

"Therefore, if anyone is in Christ,
he is a new creation.
The old has passed away;
behold, the new has come."

2 Corinthians 5:17 ESV

FREEDOM.

Freedom to love, freedom to live,
freedom to believe and achieve,
freedom from the cares of life,
freedom from envy and strife,
freedom from our failures and fears,
freedom from our trials and tears,
freedom from our shameful past,
freedom that will forever last.

Our souls long for its embrace;
our hearts yearn to know such grace.
We have searched for it in many places;
some even try to find it behind many faces.
Where can we find freedom?
It is only found in God's kingdom!
Not from the west, nor from the east,
Not from the great, nor from the least.

God's kingdom is the true land of the free;
it is the promised land to you and me.
"Whom the Son sets free is free indeed,"
regardless of background, color, or creed.
Blessed are those who for freedom thirst!
Blessed are those who seek His kingdom first!
Ah! Freedom, so much of it in God's kingdom,
where all who love Him are welcome!

"As Jesus spoke these things,
many believed in Him.
So He said to the Jews
who had believed Him,
"'If you continue in My word,
you are truly My disciples.
Then you will know the truth,
and the truth will set you free.'"

John 8:30-32 BSB

I AM ZACCHAEUS.

Zacchaeus, hurry down from the tree;
make haste, I am here to set you free.
Look, I've come to sit and dine with you;
yes I have come to make you all brand new.

Lord, how did You know my name?
I have done things that brought me shame.
I've heard that here You would pass through,
I only meant to catch a glimpse of You.

I am the Lord who sees every sparrow;
who also made your bones and marrow.
I know you are cunning and very smart,
but I have come to fill your empty heart.

How have I gained my Lord's favor?
Oh what sweet grace I now savor!
I once was weak, but now I am strong,
I will make right my every wrong!

Let's go to your house and have some food;
I am delighted to know you will do good.
You no longer need this tree called sycamore,
you are now free to live and sin no more.

Come, all you men I've stolen from,
take everything, take all, and then some!
The Lord has opened my once blinded eyes;
now I see and no more listen to the liar's lies.

‿╯‿

"But Zacchaeus stood up and said to the Lord,
"'Look, Lord, half of my possessions I give to the poor,
and if I have cheated anyone, I will repay it fourfold.'"
Jesus said to him, "'Today salvation has come to this house,
because this man too is a son of Abraham.
For the Son of Man came to seek and to save the lost.'"

Luke 19:8-10 BSB

THE TRUTH.

The truth alone is my trusted friend;
it is unchangeable and never betrays;
it is also transparent and loyal to the end.
The truth is what my soul needs always.

The truth is the language of sincere love;
it keeps the heart free, fearless, and pure;
it is passionate, fair, and gentle like a dove.
The truth ends my doubts and keeps me sure.

The truth is the currency of the humble,
the strength and wisdom of the wise;
it is the reason why liars continually stumble.
The truth is my guide and the light of my eyes.

"For I was overjoyed when the brothers came
and testified about your devotion to the truth,
in which you continue to walk.
I have no greater joy than to hear that my children
are walking in the truth."

3 John 1:3-4 BSB

TELL ME
THE TRUTH.

Relationships are beautiful,
until trust is broken;
and truth is not at all useful,
unless it is spoken.

Why are we so afraid of,
what we desperately need?
Truth is a token of love,
and a close friend indeed.

Truth is never shallow,
it can be tough to chew;
and sometimes hard to swallow,
but setting us free is what it'll do.

Slap me awake with the truth,

do not affirm me with a lie;

though I have quite a sweet tooth,

make not the truth an apple pie.

It may be bitter to my taste,

yet it is vital to my heart.

My time, please do not waste,

tell me the truth from the start.

"Therefore each of you must put off falsehood

and speak truthfully to his neighbor,

for we are all members of one another."

Ephesians 4:25 BSB

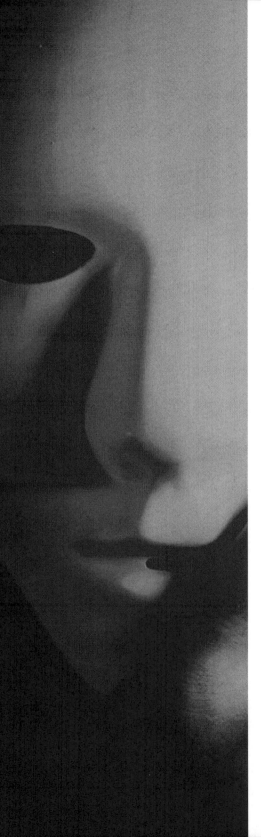

LIES.

Lies,

lies

upon

lies.

Lies,

this

world's

demise.

Lies,

huge

piles

of lies

before my troubled eyes;
all of which I so despise.

"If anyone says, '"I know Him,"'
but does not keep His commandments,
he is a liar, and the truth is not in him."

1 John 2:4 BSB

TRANSPARENCY.

My life is like an open book,
for all who wish to take a look.
I have nothing at all to hide,
I have laid down my pride.

I am delighted to decrease,
so Christ in me might increase.
I am not ashamed to let Him show;
in fact, I want everyone to know.

I am not who I used to be;
may it be clear for all to see.
I died to my sinful past,
and now I am free at last.

Though I am far from perfection,
yet I hold dear my salvation.
This has nothing to do with me,
it's Christ in me, my hope of glory.

He turned my despair into hope;
He brought far near like a telescope.
I have to walk by faith and not by sight;
Jesus will always be my guiding Light.

He has made me glad to be who I am;
now I praise Him in this poetic jam.
It is always good to be oneself;
or else, this book should stay on the shelf.

"And we all, with unveiled face,
beholding the glory of the Lord,
are being transformed into the same image
from one degree of glory to another.
For this comes from the Lord who is the Spirit."
2 Corinthians 3:18 ESV

EXPOSED.

Perhaps the man I have become
is the man I have always been,
and I was just unknown to myself?
My evil heart has been exposed;
my troubled eyes stare at it,
and I am ashamed and terrified.
O Lord, your light cuts through me
like a sharp burning blade.
You test my heart and mind,
and my thoughts and lips
reveal the wretched man I am.
In the presence of my sinful self,
my many good intentions melt away.
I can only run for so long,
and I can only go so far.
O Lord, deliver me from myself.
Let your truth be my sword,
Your righteousness my strength,
and Your love my refuge.

"'Can a man hide in secret places where I cannot see him?'" declares the LORD. "'Do I not fill the heavens and earth?'" declares the LORD."

Jeremiah 23:24 BSB

DIVINE
REMEDY.

Oh, how my heart longs to be pure!
How I crave for the divine cure!
You see, I was born infected with sin,
this stubborn deadly virus from within.

It follows me like my own shadow,
or like an old lover refusing to let go.
Always calling and pulling at my desire,
wanting to draw me near the lake of fire;
claiming to bring pleasure and joy,
all the while -my life- it seeks to destroy.

Who can rescue me from this death trap?
Who is able to -my soul- unwrap?
I thank Almighty God for His Son Jesus,
His extravagant gift of love to us.
He is the author and substance of my hope,
Who alone can save me from sin's slippery slope.

"So this is the principle I have discovered:

When I want to do good,

evil is right there with me.

For in my inner being I delight in God's law.

But I see another law at work in my body,

warring against the law of my mind

and holding me captive to the law of sin

that dwells within me.

What a wretched man I am!

Who will rescue me from this body of death?

Thanks be to God, through Jesus Christ our Lord!

So then, with my mind I serve the law of God,

but with my flesh I serve the law of sin."

Romans 7:21-25 BSB

THE BEST
GIFT .

He took upon Himself my well deserved condemnation;

His altruistic and marvelous deed produced my salvation.

What shall I return to Him for His incomparable grace?

I will give thanks to my Lord and gaze upon His face!

No measure of works of my hands will ever suffice;

a grateful and humble heart will be my worthy sacrifice.

I will declare His love forever- and of it- always sing;

I will keep my eyes fixed on Jesus, my glorious King.

"How can I repay the LORD

for all His goodness to me?

I will lift the cup of salvation

and call on the name of the LORD."

Psalm 116:12-13 BSB

MY PLACE
IN THE SON.

What bitter, yet sweet divine calamity

which has so graciously befallen me!

Painfully You have opened my eyes

to see and realize where true worth lies.

You rushed over me like mighty water falls,

and have so swiftly broken down my walls.

I surrender as I am subdued by Your might,

for I have lost my strength and desire to fight.

Now I seek no more the place where I belong;

I found it in Him who's been with me all along.

I give no regard to the status quo and all the rest;

in Christ I stand and that is where I'm at my best.

"More than that, I count all things as loss
compared to the surpassing excellence
of knowing Christ Jesus my Lord,
for whom I have lost all things.
I consider them rubbish,
that I may gain Christ."

Philippians 3:8 BSB

FAITH
RENEWAL.

Return to the Lord;
Oh my weary soul!
Return to His word,
and be again made whole.

Hope in His faithfulness;
He will see you through.
Lean on His tenderness;
He truly cares for you.

Forget not, my soul, forget not
His marvelous deeds and ways;
though painful be now your lot,
remember He is with you always.

Look up and be not afraid;
no evil against you will succeed.
Thus Your God and Maker said,
and all He speaks is true indeed.

"The LORD is good to those who wait for Him,

to the soul who seeks Him.

It is good to wait quietly

for the salvation of the LORD."

Lamentation 3:25-26 BSB

NEVER MIND.

Where should I look for peace of mind,
or sweet rest for my tired soul?
I hear it's costly and hard to find;
is it somewhere at the North Pole?

Never mind, never mind, never mind!
I found it in Jesus, my Prince of Peace.
I am going through life's daily grind,
with Jesus' peace, my sweet release.

Troubles abound and weigh me down;
my mind's racing a million miles an hour.
The devil's trying to run me out of town,
but in me resides God's mighty power.

Never mind, never mind, never mind!
I found it in Jesus, my Prince of Peace.
I am going through life's daily grind,
with Jesus' peace, my sweet release.

I am standing here in my God's grace;
the enemy's weapons have been broken.
I won't be moved from my rightful place;
"It is done!" My Savior's words spoken.

Never mind, never mind, never mind!
I found it in Jesus, my Prince of Peace.
I am going through life's daily grind,
with Jesus' peace, my sweet release.

"Peace I leave with you;
my peace I give to you.
Not as the world gives
do I give to you.
Let not your hearts be troubled,
neither let them be afraid."
John 14:27 ESV

HOMAGE
TO GOD'S LAMB.

You carried the dreadful bloody cross,
as You walked the shameful path to Calvary.
You came to win and save the lost,
despising the shame, You carried on to victory.

Lord, You have gone all the way;
You went as far as the gloomy grave.
You knew the price You had to pay,
for sinful souls of men to save.

Death could not hold You for too long;
You rose again to seal our eternal fate.
You made aright all we've done wrong,
and taught us to choose love instead of hate.

Now we behold the unfolding of all You foretold;
the earth aches and agitates, yearning for her King;
lawlessness multiplies as many hearts grow cold;
but to Your steadfast saving arms, oh Lord, we cling.

"O death, where is your victory?
O death, where is your sting?
The sting of death is sin,
and the power of sin is the law.
But thanks be to God,
who gives us the victory
through our Lord Jesus Christ."

1 Corinthians 15:55-56 ESV

ROCK N ROLL.

Justified in the Lord and saved from sin's abuse,
my soul is thoroughly untied and I am forever loose.
Elegantly clothed with His grace and righteousness,
I move in the rhythm of His love and tenderness.
Receiving sustaining grace from His sacred scroll,
I stand on my salvation Rock and this is how I roll.

"But when Christ had offered for all time
a single sacrifice for sins,
He sat down at the right hand of God.
For by a single offering He has perfected
for all time those who are being sanctified."

Hebrews 10:12,14 ESV

GOD IS IN CONTROL.

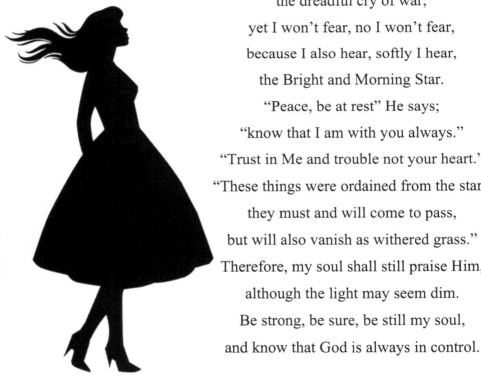

Be still, my soul, be still,

fear not and be not anxious;

believe in God's perfect will,

so pure and so precious.

But I hear, repeatedly I hear,

the dreadful cry of war;

yet I won't fear, no I won't fear,

because I also hear, softly I hear,

the Bright and Morning Star.

"Peace, be at rest" He says;

"know that I am with you always."

"Trust in Me and trouble not your heart."

"These things were ordained from the start;

they must and will come to pass,

but will also vanish as withered grass."

Therefore, my soul shall still praise Him,

although the light may seem dim.

Be strong, be sure, be still my soul,

and know that God is always in control.

"I have said these things to you,
that in Me you may have peace.
In the world you will have tribulation.
But take heart; I have overcome the world."

John 16:33 ESV

REMEMBER
LOT'S WIFE.

When you refuse to let it go,

though you know you must do so,

remember Lot's wife;

into a pillar of salt she turned,

as for her previous life she yearned.

What has been done is done.

What has been gone is gone.

Remember Lot's wife!

Do not stay stuck in this old place;

there is more ahead in God's grace.

Now must begin a new chapter;
it's okay to not know what comes after.
Remember Lot's wife!
Into God's hands leave all your fears,
He'll care for you and dry your tears.

Listen, dear child of heaven's King,
the God to whom I tightly cling.
Remember Lot's Wife!
Do not your own future concede,
by looking back as you proceed.

"But Lot's wife looked back,
and she became a pillar of salt."

Genesis 19:26 BSB

LETTING GO.

It is never easy to let "it" go;
yet letting "it" go, we must,
if we should ever learn to grow,
and not turn from dust to rust.

We are never by pain defined;
like fire purifies and refines gold,
we are indeed by pain refined;
this is a sound saying from of old.

There is a glorious side to pain;
letting go is necessary to get there.
Humility would break off our chain,
if to ourselves we would be truly fair.

"Do not call to mind the former things;
pay no attention to the things of old.
Behold, I am about to do something new;
even now it is coming. Do you not see it?
Indeed, I will make a way in the wilderness
and streams in the desert."

Isaiah 43:18-19 BSB

FEELINGS
& FAITH.

I feel like an unhinged door,
barely hanging on,
but I've been here before
and helped by the Holy One.

I feel like a parched desolate land,
scorched by the devil's heat,
but I am refreshed by God's caring hand,
from Whom comes my every heart beat.

I feel like a scattered mess,
spread across the ocean floor;
yet in the pain of my brokenness,
I know God will my soul restore.

I feel like a restless ghost,
in search of an abiding place,
but what I hope and long for most,
is to see and kiss my Father's face.

"Why are you cast down, O my soul,
and why are you in turmoil within me?
Hope in God; for I shall again
praise Him, my salvation."

Psalm 42:5 ESV

NEVER TOO FAR

So loving You are,
far from descriptions.
You're never too far,
from my afflictions.

When I need a friend,
You are always there;
a friend to the end,
You constantly care.

Purest Light divine,
hope of tomorrow,
please upon me shine,
comfort my sorrow.

Help this burdened heart,

with the cares of life,

destined from the start,

to know pain and strife.

Lord my strong tower,

It's in You I trust;

Your awesome power,

has made me from dust.

In this I will rest,

though the trials get rough,

this truth I attest,

Your grace is enough.

"The LORD is with you when you are with Him.

If you seek Him, He will be found by you,

but if you forsake Him, He will forsake you."

2 Chronicles 15:2b BSB

GOD
OUR PILLOW.

We rest our heads on God our pillow,
and more and more His love we know.
His righteousness He will us show,
and His grace on us bestow,
so that in Him we stronger grow.
As we sojourn in this world below,
His humble path we must follow;
His seeds of hope we ought to sow.
We need not fear of tomorrow,
nor of the things that bring sorrow.
Abide, abide under His shadow;
in His strong arms our cares we throw,
for our God has broken the enemy's bow,
and made His Living River in us to flow.

"Humble yourselves, therefore,
under the mighty hand of God
so that at the proper time
He may exalt you,
casting all your anxieties on Him,
because He cares for you."

1 Peter 5:6-7 ESV

TO HIS WILL
I BOW.

Long and painful may be the night,
but renewal comes in the morning.
All my darkness turns into light,
as I fix my eyes upon Jesus my King.

My journey's path is hard and narrow,
and the pain is deep and palpable;
still I press on to a brighter tomorrow,
trusting in the One who is infallible.

The Author is not yet done with my story;
it is a rough and messy draft right now.
The end will be for my good and His glory;
hence to His perfect will, I humbly bow.

"And we know that for those who love God
all things work together for good,
for those who are called
according to his purpose."

Romans 8:28 ESV

DID GOD
HAVE HIS
WAY?

Another day is forever gone
and never ever will return.
Just how much did I get done,
and what new things did I learn?

Did I use well these vanished hours?
Am I satisfied with my labor?
Did I notice and smell the flowers?
Was I kind and fair to my neighbor?

The answers may elude and scatter,
as I briefly pause to ponder my day.
In the end, here's the heart of the matter,
that is to say, did God have His way?

"Let me hear in the morning of Your steadfast love, for in You I trust. Make me know the way I should go, for to You I lift up my soul."

Psalm 143:8 ESV

CLOCK
WISE.

Mistakes will be made,
prices will be paid,
stories will be told,
just as we grow old.

Lessons must be learned,
pages must be turned,
as earth, sun, and moon;
for the end comes soon.

Was all our time spent
for what it was meant?
Theirs only—is life's prize,
those who live clock wise.

"Pay careful attention, then, to how you walk,
not as unwise but as wise, redeeming the time,
because the days are evil.
Therefore do not be foolish,
but understand what the Lord's will is."

Ephesians 5:15-17 BSB

IT'S
TIME.

It's time to be all God made me to be;

it's time to live in the plan He has for me.

No more looking back and sideways,

I'm looking ahead for the rest of my days.

Time has grown tired of waiting for me;

there is no denying this sense of urgency.

I feel like Esther, born for such a time as this;

unless I move in faith, I fear His call I'll miss.

"For if you remain silent at this time,
relief and deliverance for the Jews
will arise from another place,
but you and your father's house will perish.
And who knows if perhaps you have come
to the kingdom for such a time as this?"

Esther 4:14 BSB

SPARE ME.

Spare me your fancy flattering songs,
spare me your silly shouts of praise,
spare me your claps and noisy gongs,
spare me your empty hands upraised.

Spare me your presumptuous romance,
spare me your talent shows and offerings,
spare me your serenade and your dance,
since you ignore the poor in their sufferings.

Have I not shown you what true love is,
when I laid down my life for your sake?
When you show care for the least of these,
in this, verily, great joy and pleasure I take.

"Then the righteous will answer Him,
"'Lord, when did we see You hungry and feed You,
or thirsty and give You something to drink?
When did we see You a stranger and take You in,
or naked and clothe You?
When did we see You sick or in prison and visit You?'"
And the King will reply, 'Truly I tell you,
whatever you did for one of the least
of these brothers of Mine, you did for Me.'"

Matthew 25:37-40 BSB

LET
MONEY
BE.

As the Amazon River flows,
money comes and money goes.
Money is a tool in life's tool box
that sometimes tricks like a fox.

Money can be elusive like a ghost,
especially when chased after the most.
It is the offspring of human energy,
not that of slothfulness, or lethargy.

Don't ever fall in love with money,
it will not taste as sweet as honey.
Your sorrows will be more than doubled,
and your heart plundered and troubled.

Let money be simply money,
purposeful, good, agile and free;
or else, you will wear it like a yoke,
and soon stop breathing as you choke.

"Jesus told him, "'If you want to be perfect, go, sell your possessions and give to the poor, and you will have treasure in heaven. Then come, follow Me.'"

When the young man heard this, he went away in sorrow, because he had great wealth.

Then Jesus said to His disciples, "'Truly I tell you, it is hard for a rich man to enter the kingdom of heaven.'"

Matthew 19:21-23 BSB

THE ONLY
PURE SOURCE.

I drink from only one spiritual source;
Jesus, the Living Water, of course.
Though with falsehood society be rife,
still He is my Way, my Truth, my Life.

He is the sound wisdom of the ages,
the rejected truth of life's torn pages.
He is the cure to our self inflicted woes,
the victory over all our deadly foes.

Since you've tasted that the Lord is good,
having done for you what He alone could;
let go of your sorcery and your deception,
and keep yourself in the Lord's reception.

If you think that the Lord can be mocked,
then your access to Him will be blocked.
You may think I am crazy or simply weird,
but wisdom begins when the Lord is revered.

"When you enter the land the LORD your God is giving you,
do not imitate the detestable ways of the nations there.
Let no one be found among you who sacrifices his son
or daughter in the fire, practices divination or conjury,
interprets omens, practices sorcery, casts spells,
consults a medium or familiar spirit, or inquires of the dead.
For whoever does these things is detestable to the LORD.
And because of these detestable things,
the LORD your God is driving out the nations before you.
You must be blameless before the LORD your God."

Deuteronomy 18:9-13 BSB

TRUE WORDS
TO LIVE BY.

Love is the key of life.

Avoid envy and strife.

Walk in the grace of God,

His ways are never flawed.

Beware of bad company,

true friends are not many.

Dare to rise above.

Dare to show your love.

You'll know pain and fears,

you'll cry and shed tears,

but God will be with you;

He will see you through.

Joy comes in the morning,

and your heart will again sing.

"You have heard that it was said,

"'Love your neighbor and hate your enemy.'"

But I tell you, love your enemies

and pray for those who persecute you,

that you may be sons of your Father in heaven.

He causes His sun to rise on the evil and the good,

and sends rain on the righteous and the unrighteous."

Matthew 5:43-45 BSB

LET
LOVE.

Love must always be sincere,
or love is just another word here.
It must always be true and pure;
that is the only way it can endure.

Love is the conduit of right living;
it is strong, patient and forgiving.
Do not let love ever pass you by;
open your heart and you'll see why.

The world runs much better on love,
the purest energy from heaven above.
Let it be the force that moves you,
regardless what you may go through.

Love isn't bound by color, class or wall;
it is the greatest gift ever given to all.
Let love be what God meant it to be,
transparent, honest, humble and free.

"Love must be sincere. Detest what is evil;
cling to what is good.
Be devoted to one another in brotherly love.
Outdo yourselves in honoring one another."

Romans 12:9-10 BSB

LOVE.

Love
believes,
endures,
conquers,
restores,
rejoices,
remains,
grows.

"Love is patient,

love is kind.

It does not envy,

it does not boast,

it is not proud.

It is not rude,

it is not self-seeking,

it is not easily angered,

it keeps no account of wrongs.

Love takes no pleasure in evil,

but rejoices in the truth.

It bears all things,

believes all things,

hopes all things,

endures all things."

1 Corinthians 13:4-7 BSB

THE FRUIT
OF THE SPIRIT.

Love, like oxygen, is indispensable.

Joy will keep us steady and sensible.

Peace stabilizes the soul when afraid.

Patience is a character no one can upbraid.

Kindness honors everyone, young and old.

Goodness outlasts all seasons, hot or cold.

Faithfulness leads us to God's secret place.

Gentleness tells all that we know His grace.

Self-control will help us to finish the race.

"But the fruit of the Spirit is love, joy, peace, patience, kindness, goodness, faithfulness, gentleness, and self-control.
Against such things there is no law."

Galatians 5:22-23 BSB

THE BELL OF LOVE RINGS.

The bell of love is pleadingly ringing,
calling everyone to service and sacrifice.
The gift of hope we must all be bringing;
and reflect Christ who paid the greatest price.
Some might consider and deeply ponder,
as to what could be this greatest price?
Hear now the answer and no more wonder;
it is selfless love, nothing else will suffice.

"This is my commandment, that you love one another as I have loved you. Greater love has no one than this, that someone lay down his life for his friends. "

John 15:12-13 ESV

LOVE MOVED OUT.

I went over to the house of Love,
I found out He no longer lives there.
Forced out with a subtle shove,
He moved to some place somewhere.

But this place is just a heart away;
hopefully yours, hopefully mine.
Yet this I know as night and day,
without love, no one is ever fine.

Now another lives in His once holy house,
not as a guest, but sadly as the new master.
Initiated by the idolatry of His spouse,
he now leads and continues deceiving her.

"But I have this against you:
You have abandoned your first love.
Therefore, keep in mind how far you have fallen.
Repent and perform the deeds you did at first.
But if you do not repent,
I will come to you and remove
your lampstand from its place."

Revelation 2:4-5 BSB

A LITTLE PONDERING.

What would the world look like, if the presence of evil and its influence were completely removed from the earth and the universe altogether? What would it be like if wickedness was completely removed from the heart of humanity? Would things like love, forgiveness, mercy, and compassion become extinct, or unnecessary? You know, kind of, would pain medicine become extinct if pain was to stop existing? Are these things merely coping, or defense mechanisms for humanity to prevent self destruction? These questions stop here for me as my pondering is satisfied with this truth; in the end, only one thing will remain, while all others vanish; this one thing is none other than love. Yes, love in absolute perfection. Therefore, I conclude that love is humanity's highest calling. Let us answer the call.

"Now we see but a dim reflection as in a mirror; then we shall see face to face. Now I know in part; then I shall know fully, even as I am fully known. And now these three remain: faith, hope, and love; but the greatest of these is love."

1 Corinthians 13:12-13 BSB

DELIGHTFUL MORNING.

Gently awaken with a kiss by the morning light,

I rise to a new day filled with joy and beauty in sight;

serenaded with pure melodious sounds of God's love,

soft and tender rhythmic whispers descending from above.

So harmonious, the angelic voices flowing as a water stream,

refresh and cheer my soul, then bid my heart to dream.

Amazed, I gaze upon the immense blue sky

and wish for eagle's wings that I may fly.

"This is the day that the LORD has made;
we will rejoice and be glad in it."

Psalm 118:24 BSB

LOOK AND LISTEN.

Look at the happy trees dancing,
dancing to the rhythm of the wind;
wind so gentle and entrancing,
entrancing and soothing without end.

Listen to the lovely birds singing,
singing their sweetest song;
song composed for a fair King,
King of all that's true and strong.

Look at the light in this man's eyes,
eyes that shine with great delight;
delight reserved only for the wise,
wise to notice such sound and sight.

Listen to the beating of his heart,
heart beating five thousand beats,
beats per hour and start after start,
start of the cycle of sweet repeats.

"He has made everything beautiful in its time.
He has also set eternity in the hearts of men,
yet they cannot fathom the work that God
has done from beginning to end."

Ecclesiastes 3:11 BSB

CONSIDER THE SPARROW.

{A Tanka}

I love the sparrow,
for we are so much alike–
in this world's grand schemes;
yet as hard as I may try,
I cannot escape His eyes.

"Are not two sparrows sold for a penny?
Yet not one of them will fall to the ground
apart from the will of your Father."

Matthew 10:29 BSB

SUMMER.

You were right there at my birth,
to welcome me upon the earth.
I have known you since day one;
being with you is so much fun.

Summer, I'm glad you're back at last;
the previous year was such a blast.
You are so beautiful and warm;
I love your company and charm.

My toes are super glad you're here;
my sandals welcome you with cheer;
my short pants rejoice to see you;
because they're free to move anew.

It is time to activate the cooking grill,
sit on the porch to contemplate and chill.
It's time to hit the swimming pool;
I don't mean literally just like a fool.

Summer, you radiate the Creator's smile;
you make my days bright and worthwhile.
Welcome back, my sweet friend summer;
life without you can often be a bummer.

But please don't tell the others I said that.
Winter might get mad and hit me with a bat;
she tends to get jealous, moody and cold.
Keep this as our secret, one that's never told.

"To everything there is a season,
and a time for every purpose under heaven."

Ecclesiastes 3:1 BSB

WHERE WILD FLOWERS GROW.

A lonely garden of bitterness,
where only wild flowers grow;
longing for rain of happiness,
instead showered with sorrow.

Such is the sadly broken heart,
where pain and anger rule;
hoping for love that won't depart,
to fill the void so deep and cruel.

Please do your heart this one favor,
give time and forgiveness a chance;
you'll some day taste true love's flavor,
and changed will be your circumstance.

AUTHOR'S NOTE:

Wild flowers in this poem represent despair, resentment, confusion, rage, suicidal thoughts, etc.

"Guard your heart with all diligence,
for from it flow springs of life."

Proverbs 4:33 BSB

REST.

{Haiku.}

Come to Me My child.

Let your heart rest in My love;

all you need is faith.

"Come to Me, all you who are weary and burdened, and I will give you rest."

Matthew 11:28 BSB

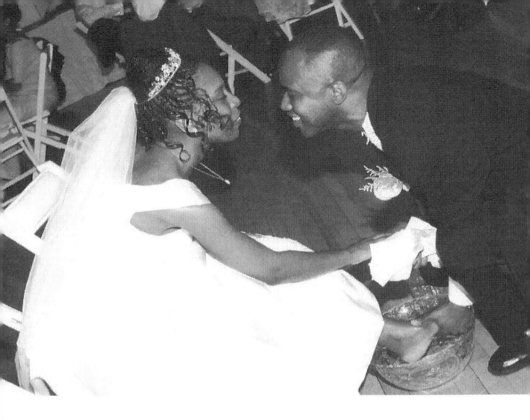

WHAT ABOUT US?

Darling, do you remember our first date?
Hand in hand, we strolled in Prospect Park,
talking, laughing, and singing until late;
it mattered not at all it became dark.

Darling, do you remember our first kiss?
It was sweetly strange and super fast.
How can I forget this unexpected bliss,
which came and went in a humorous blast?

We talked about Esther's brave young heart;
how she was born for such a divine cause.
She trusted God and played well her part,
saving her people's lives from death's jaws.

What about us, my dear sister and bride,
what is the cause for which we were born?
Why have we been joined to each other's side?
Isn't it to serve Him, who for our sins was torn?

Together we have covered plenty of ground–
on a path that is indeed hard and narrow.
May we never lose sight of the treasures found,
in Him whose eyes rest upon every sparrow.

~

"For we are God's workmanship,
created in Christ Jesus to do good works,
which God prepared in advance as our way of life."

Ephesians 2:10 BSB

HAIKU
INSPECTOR.

Here you go again,

counting all my syllables.

Are you happy now?

⌣

"He will yet fill your mouth with laughter,
and your lips with a shout of joy."

Job 8:21 BSB

RELAXATION.
{Haiku}

Close your eyes and then,
from the vast supply of air,
breathe, keep breathing, there.

"Return to your rest, O my soul,
for the LORD has been good to you."

Psalm 116:7 BSB

ELEVATE.

{Senryū}

Don't reciprocate
this degrading thing called hate;
instead, elevate.

"If anyone claims to be in the light
but hates his brother,
he is still in the darkness."

1 John 2:9 BSB

EVOLVING EVIL

Evil is like an ever growing wild fire–

raging through the forest of humanity,

intent on destroying all good things in its path.

This fire seems hopelessly hard to combat,

or contain; let alone conquer. Why?

Because it burns deep within the forest

of the human heart.

"Do not be overcome by evil,
but overcome evil with good."

Romans 12:21 BSB

MY CHILD

I've waited for you, my child
like the morning dew, my child
if you really knew, my child
what I have gone through, my child

you would come to me, my child
so you would be free, my child
from iniquity, my child
and your eyes would see, my child

as clear as sky's blue, my child
what I had to do, my child
to make you anew, my child
oh how I love you, my child

we are family, my child

irreversibly, my child

for eternity, my child

you belong to me, my child.

"And the son said to him, 'Father,

I have sinned against heaven and before you.

I am no longer worthy to be called your son.'

But the father said to his servants,

'Bring quickly the best robe, and put it on him,

and put a ring on his hand, and shoes on his feet.

And bring the fattened calf and kill it,

and let us eat and celebrate.

For this my son was dead, and is alive again;

he was lost, and is found.'

And they began to celebrate."

Luke 15:21-24 ESV

YOU
MATTER.

{Haiku.}

You are a blessing,
bestowed to earth from heaven;
you really matter.

"Children are indeed a heritage from the LORD,
and the fruit of the womb is His reward."

Psalm 127:3 BSB

I WILL MAKE IT
THROUGH.

Please let me fly upon Your gentle wings,

upon the wings of your Spirit and Your love;

then I will be capable to face all things,

things from below and things from above.

I will fly right through the thick dark clouds,

I will jump through lightning like rope,

I will subdue my fears, wrap'em up in shrouds,

for on Your wings I'd catch the ray of hope.

"He will cover you with His feathers;
you will take refuge under His wings.
His faithfulness will be a protective shield."

Psalm 91:4 KJV

YOUR ATTENTION, PLEASE.

Listen to the sound of My pleading voice,

voice calling fervently for your attention;

attention to ask you to make the choice,

choice to live your life as not in detention.

It's time to reveal what you're made of,

of divine power, creativity and dreams;

dreams to fulfill by faith, hope, and love,

love flowing from Me like gentle streams.

Listen to the sound of My singing voice,

voice singing over you the sweetest melody;

melody bidding your heart to trust and rejoice,

rejoice that you are blessed and called by Me.

"The LORD your God is among you;
He is mighty to save.
He will rejoice over you with gladness;
He will quiet you with His love;
He will rejoice over you with singing."

Zephaniah 3:17 BSB

ATLANTA.

Amazing and delightful to the sight,
is America's radiant southern light.
She is the city of daring dreamers,
the city of hope and truth screamers.

She birthed the great prophet of love,
the fearless Dr. King, gentle as a dove.
She is the city of Nobel Prize winners,
the city of diverse saints and sinners.

"The eyes of the LORD are in every place,
keeping watch on the evil and the good."

Proverbs 15:3 ESV

BE READY TO FLY.

Can you hear the last trumpet's blast?
Do you know how long it will last?
Can you see the writing on the wall?
Can you hear the Lord's final call?

The great King of glory will soon be here
to gather His elect from far and near.
So lift up your heads and keep'm up high;
spread wide your wings and be ready to fly.

"Then we who are alive, who are left,
will be caught up together with them
in the clouds to meet the Lord in the air,
and so we will always be with the Lord."

1 Thessalonians 4:17 ESV

TO BE IN GOD'S PRESENCE:

I stepped out onto the deck of my house one morning to pray. I could not help but marvel at the lovely sky and the majestically tall handsome trees for a brief moment. The birds sang jovially and beautifully as usual. In gratitude I lifted up my voice to the sky and thanked God for giving me eyes to see and ears to hear the beauty of His creation. Suddenly I was interrupted by this indescribably wonderful feeling which came over me and brought me to joyful tears. I felt like I was in His presence and that He heard everything I said. I can't tell you just how much this mattered to my soul. There have been many other times when I have experienced this feeling during prayer. To tell you the truth, for the majority of times when I pray I do not feel anything at all. Faith is not about feeling that I am in His presence. Faith is about knowing that I am in His presence. Although, I must say that I am always grateful every time I have such an experience. The gratification that my soul feels at the sense of being close to my Creator is beyond amazing. To be in His presence is the ultimate definition of what heaven is. That morning, and at other times, I have enjoyed a delicious, tiny taste of heaven. It would be the understatement of all times to say that my soul longs for the time to be in my Father's presence forever. May He grant you and I this eternal joy.

"You make known to me the path of life;
in Your presence there is fullness of joy;
at Your right hand are pleasures forevermore."

Psalm 16:11 ESV

ABOUT THE AUTHOR:

"Every good and perfect gift comes from above, descending from the Father of lights." Poetry has indeed been a wonderful and empowering gift in my life since my teenage years. It has given me a voice and a platform to engage with the world in a profoundly meaningful and spiritual way. I am humbled and excited to share this gift with you. It is my sincere hope that your hearts will draw a little closer to God through my poetry. I am originally from Haiti. I now live in Dacula, Georgia, with my lovely wife and 2 of our 3 children; our eldest is currently studying at Cornell University. If you would like to have me come and do a reading at your church, or special event, please contact me at info@thepoetrygallery.com. You can also go to www.thepoetrygallery.com

. . . .

"And let us consider how to stir up
one another to love and good works,"
Hebrews 10:24

BLESSING:

Blessed are You O LORD, Ruler of the universe Who has sanctified us and commanded to live holy. Blessed are You Father of lights from Whom comes every good and perfect gift, and with Whom there is no change or shifting shadow. Blessed are You O LORD, Ruler of the universe who has graciously and generously blessed us with the gift of Your Son, our Lord Jesus (Yeshua) who is the Light of the world, our very Light now and forever. Amen.

Made in the USA
Columbia, SC
15 May 2021